KUNDALINI AWAKENING

DISCOVER HOW TO BOOST YOUR POSITIVE ENERGY AND RELIEVE STRESS BY ACHIEVING HIGHER LEVELS OF CONSCIOUSNESS AND REBALANCING YOUR CHAKRAS

by Athena Frazier

© Copyright 2020 Athena Frazier - All rights reserved.

The information presented in this report solely and fully represents the views of the author as of the date of publication. Any result of changing information, conditions or contexts, this author reserves the right to alter content at their sole discretion impunity.

It is illegal to copy, distribute, or create derivative works from this ebook in whole or in part. No part of this report may be reproduced or transmitted in any form whatsoever, electronic, or mechanical, including photocopying, recording, or by any informational storage or retrieval system without expressed written, dated and signed permission from the author.

TABLE OF CONTENT

Introduction 6

Chapter 1: Understanding what Kundalini is 9

Chapter 2: The history of Kundalini 22

Chapter 3: The benefits of Kundalini 31

Chapter 4: How to awaken a dormant Kundalini 37

Chapter 5: Kundalini and yoga 46

Chapter 6: The best yoga poses to awaken Kundalini 56

Chapter 7: Reaching the higher self 69

Chapter 8: Prana 74

Chapter 9: The source, Akasha 78

Chapter 10: Kundalini and Chakras 87

Chapter 11: Enhancing psychic abilities 97

Chapter 12: Astral Travel and Clairvoyance 110

Chapter 13: Activate And Decalcify Your Pineal Gland 114

Conclusion 119

Introduction

The term "Kundalini" typically refers to the dimension of energy that has not realized its potential. There is an enormous well of energy inside you that is available to be tapped. This energy source is there and awaiting you to get access to it.

You are resting upon a bounty and treasure inside. Much like a hidden treasure, we need a map or blueprint to guide us and lead us to this place.

Thus, if you know what the power is, you are on your way to begin the journey to reaching it. The second step is to understand better what this energy can do and what you can achieve from it. Once you have completed this journey, you will be connected to an endless source of power. This is what Kundalini is.

All human beings possess and innate intellectual mechanism in their genetic makeup that makes it possible for them to tap into their hidden divine power, illumination and genius. This mechanism, or energy, is called Kundalini.

The word Kundalini originates from Sanskrit and means the coiled one. In fact, in ancient Eastern religions, the energy is depicted as coiled around the vertebrae column base three times and a half like a serpent. In these etchings, the coiled serpent rouses from slumber from the vertebrae column while one is meditating deeply or praying.

In its simplest terms Kundalini is the primary energy, also known as Shakti, positioned at the spinal cord base. It is an energy that manipulates and runs the spiritual and intellectual life force (prana) of all human beings. When awakened, it promotes spiritual awakening and attaining of intellectual maturity. Though the energy is naturally present in everyone, it is not that easy to deliberately awaken it because as humans we have intellectual and spiritual blockages that hinder awakening of our kundalini

Once achieved, Kundalini awakening leads to spiritual awakening, freedom of the soul and awakening of creativity and freedom.

Chapter 1: Understanding What Kundalini Is

Kundalini is known to be the energy of the consciousness that is a spiritual-psycho energy that lives within the resting body, and that is why it needs to be awakened. The term means "annular or circular", and was also a name that was often given to snakes in the 12th century.

It originated from the yogic belief that corporeal energy is real and that it resides inside a person's body, particularly at the base of one's spine. Kundalini can be awakened if one connects with his soul and decides to seek the truth within himself.

The Kundalini represents a sleeping serpent or a goddess at one's spine where all the power and energy comes from. It is also said to be a libidinal or instinctive force.

Kundalini is a potent, fiery energy located at the bottom of each person's spine. This energy is both powerful and intelligent, and it energizes the body while heightening our consciousness. Its name derives from the Sanskrit Kundala, a word that means coiled. When dormant, the Kundalini remains coiled around the tailbone until it climbs up to the head. This awakening can happen spontaneously or voluntarily.

Awakening the Kundalini results in spiritual enlightenment, which bestows upon the person many gifts: increased strength, improved health, tranquility, bliss, wisdom, and even supernatural abilities.

Many belief systems have equated Kundalini activation with spiritual liberation and the complete fulfillment of man's potential; thus, many people are practicing techniques to rouse their own Kundalini.

The idea of the Kundalini or Shakti originates from Hinduism, but some say that it has its counterpart in other religions. For example, Christianity calls it the Holy Spirit or Pentecostal Fire, Judaism refers to it as Shekinah, in Islam it is Sakina, in Egypt its name is Sekhem, and in Gnostic traditions it is the Goddess or Divine Mother. Taoists describe it as the more significant/greatest Kan (Water) and Li (fire), the Kalahari gave it the name Num, and the Kaballists refer to it as the "secret fire".

The energy is a female energy naturally attracted to the masculine force in the top of the head or fontanel. Some consider meeting the two forces of the Divine Mother/Goddess and Divine Father/God as a sacred marriage that bears the Son of God. Furthermore, some say that Jesus has successfully ignited this spiritual fire, thus he became the Christ or anointed one. This is also the reason why he was supposedly able to perform miracles and attain a divine status.

Although some people have attached religious ideas to Kundalini, some say that it is beyond any specific religion or culture. Individuals from all kinds of backgrounds experience

Kundalini awakening deals with subtle energies (called prana, chi, orgone, etheric energy, bio energy or vital energy) and the subtle human anatomy (ex: nadis, energy meridians, chakras, auras, energy fields, etc.).

According to Hindu and many other mystical systems of belief, everything has components that are non-physical and are inaccessible to the ordinary physical senses. Instead, they are usually perceived via extra-sensory perception. At certain conditions, they can cause effects that are perceivable by senses or gadgets – like light, heat, vibration, radiation, or fluctuations in random number generator results. Kundalini is a subtle energy that resides in the subtle energy body, with the coccyx or tailbone as its physical container.

The different kinds of subtle energies have their characteristics and purposes. Kundalini in particular is thought of as a force that spurs rapid evolution. It is explained to be the driving force of a single fertilized egg transforming into billions of cells that are coordinated together to form a live human body.

After the baby has emerged from the womb, the Kundalini is still operational but in a subdued form. It may act in full force once more when the individual is genetically predisposed for it or if he/she has undergone individual experiences or spiritual practices.

When the Kundalini uncoils and awakens, it rises the spine in the form of pulses, waves, sparks, or flames. It then taps to the energies of the Universe, which enter the body to cleanse and infuse the person with power. Although this may happen spontaneously, majority of people need to undergo specific processes to make this possible.

Although it is not yet fully understood why spontaneous awakenings occur, some guess that the subconscious mind, the soul, or the Divine knows that it is the right time to activate the dormant energy. Whatever the reason may be, it will cause changes in the person's life, ultimately leading to the greater good.

Again, the essential purpose of the Kundalini is to help with evolution. It brings energy and directs the processes necessary to upgrade the individual so that he/she can cope with living at a higher level. Even when it is dormant, it still performs several functions, such as spark growth, generate sex drive and build consciousness. It energizes prana or vital energy so that it can carry sensations and impulses more effectively. However, the Kundalini only works at its fullest when it reaches the crown of the head. Because of this, a person must have a clear Kundalini path; if not, he or she has to prepare the path for the energy. Otherwise, he or she will feel pain or pressure as the energy encounters blocks, or the Kundalini may not move at all.

Energy Blockages

Kundalini awakening becomes problematic when the energy encounters blocks along its path. Blocks may form as a result of:

- negativity
- repressed emotions
- psychological wounds
- rigid beliefs and attitudes
- afflictions

- attachments
- unprepared body

These blocks limit consciousness and energy, making it harder for Kundalini to perform in its full power. Thus, Kundalini awakening practices involves clearing blocks. Spontaneous awakening happens when these issues are resolved.

According to Yogic belief, there are two energetic channels (Nadis) along the spinal column called the Ida and the Pingala, and a hollow canal (Nadi) named as the Sushumna. The Kundalini lies dormant at the bottom of this column and coiled around the tailbone three and a half times. When it stirs awake, it pushes through the channel and peels off the layers that separate the mind from the ultimate reality.

Although the Kundalini's biological basis is not yet understood, it is sometimes associated with the nervous system that comprises the brain, the spinal cord, and the multitude of nerves in the body. These physical parts help produce sensation and awareness via the help of electrical signals. Because of its functions and behavior, the Kundalini may be related to the nervous system's workings, and when the energy rises, it may pass through the spinal cord until it reaches into the brain. Once it's there, it may amplify the person's entire energy system, bestowing new abilities and empowering existing ones.

Before that happens though, it must traverse through the channels whether they are physical or energetic. Since the Kundalini is a powerful force, it can damage when it gets stuck where it isn't supposed to be. This is one crucial reason why Kundalini awakening is notoriously risky.

Because of Kundalini activation's potential dangers, many teachers warn students not to activate it without good reason, and simply being curious about it may cause regrets later on. It is best if you seek this only if you are ready to experience discomfort for the sake of refining your soul. It will also help to know more about it as much as possible, especially if you notice Kundalini activation symptoms in you already.

Symptoms of Blockages

The manifestation of blockages depends on where the Kundalini got stuck. It may feel as tightness, heat, tingling, or any kind of discomfort or unusual sensation in the body's area. Sometimes, it may affect the aspect of life that corresponds to a troublesome chakra – an excessive sex drive when it gets trapped in the sacral chakra, overthinking when it gets lost in the throat chakra.

The blockages themselves are not a permanent hindrance to the awakened Kundalini's momentum though. If it is sufficiently active, the force will simply burn through the obstacles. This may cause pain on the physical, cognitive, or emotional level depending on what the Kundalini touches. Aside from this, the Kundalini will draw on prana to sustain itself. If the area it finds itself lacks this vital energy, the fire may behave erratically.

Keep in mind that when the awakening process has begun, it is usually unstoppable. It will burn through impediments, cleanse impurities, and untangle knots in the energetic channels. It may influence your energy to experience specific events or become predisposed to certain kinds of behavior that will eventually lead to greater freedom. Thus, you must be willing to face the consequences and do your best to assist its progress.

Consider the Kundalini as an intelligent force that knows what it's doing. Do your best to understand it. If you can't comprehend it, just trust it.

Symptoms of Kundalini Awakening

Kundalini influences the body and mind so its release brings about physical and psychological symptoms. There is a wide range of Kundalini symptoms – some of them highly desirable while others cause frustration.

Body

- Involuntary movements - shaking and jerking
- Involuntary positioning - asanas (Yoga postures) and mudras (Yoga hand gestures
- Unusual sensations - tingling, itching, vibrating, crawling, electric shocks , intense heat or cold, a cool breeze, inner lightness, electric current travelling along the spine or the arms and hands

- Heightened sensitivity to lights, sounds, bodily sensations
- Restlessness
- Headaches, migraines, pressure, pains
- Increased blood pressure
- Irregular heartbeat
- Disrupted sleep pattern (insomnia or excessive sleeping)
- Disrupted eating pattern (appetite loss or binge eating)
- Disturbed digestive and excretory processes
- Increased strength
- Faster healing
- Greater body-mind coordination
- Strong resistance to illness

Emotions
- A feeling of losing control
- Diminished or increased sexual desire
- Emotional upheavals, mood swings, or numbness
- Intense desire to improve one's self and the world

- Lack of interest in socializing with others
- Bliss
- Tranquility
- Infinite love
- Connection to the universe

Mind

- Changes in perceptions
- Changes in mental function
- Unusual perceptions - visions, sounds, etc.
- Seeing lights in the environment
- Seeing auras or lights around or inside the body (clouds or flashes of colors)
- Altered states of consciousness
- Dissociation
- Depersonalization
- Absorption
- Greater sensitivity to art
- Paranormal experiences: Telepathy, prophetic dreams, visions, hearing disembodied voices and sounds

- Stronger intuition
- Developing new talents, improving old ones
- Ability to make better decisions
- Gaining a direction in life
- Expanded, heightened or deepened awareness

Intense experiences usually last from 5 to 30 minutes only. Your system will adjust itself to the higher energy level so it will gradually feel normal. If you are overwhelmed by what's happening, reduce your activity levels. Stop exercising and meditating for a while until the symptoms calm down.

These symptoms may be caused by changes in the individual's energy patterns that are brought about by the ascending Kundalini. Some have theorized that Kundalini awakening is a natural part of human evolution since it causes several people's changes. According to them, the Kundalini may serve a role in modifying the nervous system to allow the person to function in a different state of existence.

According to a 2008 study done by Sanchez and Daniels, such symptoms are common among those who practice 'transpersonal activities' – activities beyond ordinary personal concerns such as spiritual and mystic practices. These symptoms are not usually present in people who do not perform these kinds of activities.

Also, people who follow different paths may experience different symptoms, with those following 'unstructured paths' (practices that do not prescribe methods) experiencing more unpleasant symptoms than those adhering to 'structured paths' (practices with particular techniques). This means that Kundalini activation is better done intentionally and methodically. Although you can attempt activation on your own, it's best if you can find a teacher who already has an activated Kundalini.

A word of caution: awakening the Kundalini is a profound practice that involves accelerating your spiritual evolution in one lifetime so that you can meet God and attain a god-like state. Sure, it does bring benefits such as better health, psychic abilities, increased magnetism and the likes, but if you are focused on these instead of the process, the activation may not happen. Instead, concentrate on only doing what you need to to activate it. This will give you a pure mindset that's conducive for the activation.

Before anything else, be sincere in determining your reasons for rousing the serpent energy. You must put your whole heart and mind into what you're doing. If you have an internal conflict, a part of you may resist what you're trying to achieve, even to the point that it will create obstacles for you. Ponder on the things that are truly important to you and determine whether Kundalini activation is in line with that. If not, reflect on what you need to adjust.

If you sense that you're not yet ready, don't rush. The soul has all the time in the Universe. It can patiently wait for one or thousands of lifetimes more, so you don't need to feel pressured into doing it. After all, everything you do down to the most ordinary of actions will contribute to your spiritual growth. You don't need to dive into mystical practices just because you think you need to or just curious about them.

There are times when the Kundalini stirs even if you're not aware of it or are not consciously trying to activate it. In this case, it may be a signal that you're being helped with your evolution. If so, it's better if you permit it to happen and cope with the discomfort rather than attempt to stop it.

Chapter 2: The History Of Kundalini

From time immemorial, humans have been trying to understand their world and control what is in it. Artists have drawn, sang and written their interpretation of what the universe is about. Scientists have sunk a lot of time, energy and resources into research; religions have risen and fallen, all to uncover the universe's secret. Yet despite all that effort, every day something new is discovered.

However, most people forget to look at the most critical unit of the universe themselves in all these efforts. You can't understand the universe, if you do not understand yourself and haven't unlocked all the innate powers that you hold within yourself. Kundalini is one of the most potent energies of the self. Once locked it allows an individual to understand and experience their world in unimaginable ways. It allows you to exceed your spiritual, intellectual and physical limits.

The earliest mention of the word Kundalini can be traced to the Vedic writings collected. These writings were referred to as Upanishads, a word used to mean listening to the master's teachings while sitting down. During such lessons, the learners would be given oral recitations religious insights by a master while sitting down.

During this period, the records point out that Kundalini was an energy science and a divine philosophy. There was no physical component of the Kundalini. However, over time, the Upanishads' position was adopted as the official physical position during yogic activities. It is still in use today. This yoga was never taught to anyone or the public. Kundalini yoga was treated as higher learning for students who had undergone rigorous preparation to equip their bodies and minds for the soul and body instructions from their Kundalini masters.

The choice of a follower who would be taught the science of Kundalini was done in utmost secrecy. This follower had to be from the elite family and possess particular attributes that set him apart from the rest and assessed by the master in secret. Once a worthy candidate was spotted, he would be initiated into the influential Indian Yoga's secret society.

Kundalini awakening was a secret kept from the public. Practitioners thought they were doing the public a favor by not teaching them because; the public was not prepared to handle the power that was to be aroused in them if they knew. Such was the secrecy that covered Kundalini yoga practice.

In the Eleventh Century, the practice extended to Buddhism and Hinduism. Practitioners of these faiths began to experiment in Kundalini awakening to understand and unleash the immense power that lie restrained in the human body. In the Fifteenth Century, practitioners of Hatha yoga began to practice Kundalini awakening. Come the Sixteenth Century, practitioners of Upanihads Yoga began to study and practice Kundalini awakening.

For a long time, tapping into Kundalini energy remained a preserve of the few, mainly the Chinese and Indians. They guarded it as a great secret that would only be passed from a teacher to a praiseworthy and loyal student. Teaching Kundalini or even making known the secret of Kundalini awakening was a taboo and attracted a severe punishment to the perpetrator of such a sin. The practice was deemed as purely religious.

They experimented with the immense power that lay restrained in the human body through their widely practiced yoga. These communities had a persistently rich spiritual culture that sought and still seeks to streamline and purify the human body to release Kundalini that is supposed to cause a transformation of the intellect. For the Chinese Taoists, to be ushered into spiritual enlightenment, also referred to as the Tao, requires that one achieve Yin Yang stability and practice the microcosmic path.

Between 1875 and 1961, Carl Jung, a psychiatrist, began a campaign to make Western countries aware of Kundalini and the immense power that comes with his awakening. Jung's efforts were mostly successful because most of the West's interests in the energy can be traced back to him and other practitioners.

Jung and these other practitioners had experienced Kundalini awakening and had first hand information of how the energy works. Although its manifestation was different in each of them and their interpretation of the practice of Kundalini awakening was different, they were all working from one common ground; that Kundalini was an energy sleeping in the human being that could be summoned. They all believed that Kundalini could advance spiritual development in an individual, but needed to be controlled or mastered well.

Kundalini started getting so many attention in the 1970's, but research has it that a couple of people, including one of the most popular Psychologists in the world, Carl Jung, have known about it even in the early '30's, because they became familiar with Sanskrit and Greek teachings. Incidentally, Kundalini has been used as a technical term in most Shakti or Durga writings even back in the 11th century. It has been used by Yoga Upanishads to show others that they are more powerful than them.

These influential practitioners and came up with their proposals on the practice of Kundalini awakening. One of these practitioners, George King, asserted that Kundalini's total control through the vertebrae is man's ultimate mission on earth. King also tried to break down the Kundalini awakening process while citing ways to achieve safely through living a well balanced life ad devoting oneself to serving people selflessly.

Because of Jung, King and other progressives, the 60s was the decade of progression for Kundalini knowledge. No longer was it a preserve of Easterners. Many Westerners became interested in Kundalini, how to awaken it, and meditation in general. By the 1970s, Kundalini knowledge became even more popular as more people became interested in awakening their innate spiritual and intellectual powers. Driven by this need, more people were trained in awakening Kundalini the correct way and recognizing the signs that came with an awakening.

Currently, Kundalini has been adopted and can be mentioned alongside many religious terms or about specific religious organizations, especially the newly launched ones. However, science remains skeptical of the whole concept of Kundalini awakening, which quite frankly is no surprise since science is more focused on what can be seen, heard, touched, smelled or tasted. Kundalini is more about the sixth sense and what can be felt.

However, despite its skepticism, even science cannot ignore the increased interest in Kundalini awakening or the changes in people who have experienced it show. Scientists, especially those within the medical field, have been studying Kundalini to understand how it can be applied to therapy and healing. Some medical practitioners have inculcated Kundalini yoga into their routine procedures and practice it in their clinics. A lot of research has also gone into determining the link between mental stability and meditation.

The problem with this haphazard integration of Kundalini into medical therapy is that rarely are the correct awakening procedures followed. When this happens, side-effects to those being incorrectly prepared and awakened can be disastrous to say the least. There have been cases of patients suffering mental and emotional disturbances. Therefore, some medical personnel have taken this to mean that Kundalini in general is a dangerous practice that shouldn't be tried out.

Fortunately, as the practice of Kundalini awakening grows, more and more information about Kundalini awakening is being disseminated to the public. The issue is that most of the disseminated information speaks to what the awakening is but does not go deeper into the issue explaining the step-by-step process of awakening or what to do afterwards. You're in luck because in this guide I've tried to explain these steps as well as how to do them safely.

Reality or Metaphorical Legend?

While there is no concrete proof regarding whether Kundalini is metaphorical or absolute, the information and opinions formed are based on personal experiences. This makes proving or disproving the existence of its force difficult, at best. Individuals who are enlightened by Kundalini energy or awareness may have differing spiritual or obscure experiences. According to Hatha Yoga, the force and energy of Kundalini exists in your spine base and until stimulated (by a variety of means, exhibiting numerous sensations and responses) it hangs out in a dormant state. Yogi Bhajan expresses in his book, Kundalini, Evolution and Enlightenment, "Kundalini is the creative potential in the man".

The single, common factor among people who encounter the internal force is that each one has an awareness that gives them a deep insight into their own subtle body and soul. The subtle body comprises the mind, spiritual and energetic imprints, the sequence patterns, and order of energies within an individual.

Additionally, the obscure, subtle body encompasses any emotional or internal barriers.

Regardless of medical professionals' opinion or doubt from 'non-believers', some individuals have a strong inner confidence in their belief that Kundalini does exist. For those people who have experienced the arousal or awakening of their Kundalini energy, whether in a positive, negative, planned, or unexpected sense, they have reported feelings and sensations that are so intense that, in their minds, there is no possibility that the spiritual occurrence could be metaphorical nor imagined.

Acceptance / Non-Acceptance

Kundalini is not a medically supported phenomenon. There are no doctors who are ever going to find scientific evidence that substantiates Kundalini's presence or existence and the energy triggered by its occurrence.

There are advocates for Kundalini who claim that a typical human being used about 1 to 2% of their brain potential, while individuals who have encountered total enlightenment through Kundalini awakening use the entire 100%.

Some medical professionals have gone as far as to say that psychotic episodes among individuals practicing yoga to arouse Kundalini energy are just related health issues or concerns. Although there are some valid concerns in regards to adverse effects, most yoga practitioners who work with people trying to find or awaken there energy would agree that the adverse incidents are most likely to occur when the individual does not follow the set instructions and take their time, trying to reach Kundalini awareness at a far too rapid pace.

Regardless of the beliefs or 'success stories' told by yoga practitioners and individuals who have experienced the effects or sensations of arousing Kundalini energy, the energy and release are spiritual events related to the mind and soul. In contrast, medical professionals seek factual events related to the body, bones, organs, and nervous and circulatory systems.

Chapter 3: The Benefits of Kundalini

Many people assume that Kundalini awakening is for the spiritual fanatics or for people who practice Eastern religions. The truth is that everyone can experience immense benefits from awakening their Kundalini. Awakening your Kundalini is akin to activating a life force within your body; a life force that is the source of genius, creativity and psychic gifts. But what exactly does that mean in layman's terms?

Well for one, Kundalini enhances your connection with the central power you believe in. For instance, many people who pray report that it is more an automatic thing for them and that as they pray they often feel as if they are praying to empty air. However, once your Kundalini is awakened you'll feel a new spiritual connection with your God. That 'empty' feeling will no longer be there because you can feel your God's presence within and around you.

When you can communicate more actively with the source of your beliefs, it also makes it much easier to follow your religion's tenets. Tasks like prayer, following commandments or rules becomes much, much more comfortable. You'll find yourself living a much more natural lifestyle where you are honest about who you are, your weaknesses and your strengths.

When you can be honest about who you are then it makes accepting yourself that much more accessible and changing the habits you don't like about yourself much more comfortable. When you accept yourself, you already know what your likes and dislikes are and who you are genuinely within and are therefore less likely to conform to other people's perceptions of who you are.

This honest approach to living is also better for you and the people around you. An awakening will make it easier for you to determine which people you need in your life and which relationships you need to wean yourself out of. It helps you better appreciate the quality relationships you have and make it easier to tend these relationships with love for a more fulfilling life.

This pragmatic approach to life extends beyond better knowledge of self and better relationships. It also makes it much easier to deal with the troubles, tribulations, and unexpected daily life occurrences. It is doubtful to see someone who has experienced an awakening being over-emotional.

For instance, if public speaking gave you anxiety attacks before the awakening, you may find yourself suddenly calmer. There have been reported cases of people with anger problems suddenly becoming more controlled and less likely to explode. Situations like death, sickness and breakups don't seem to affect you as much. Of course, this doesn't mean you don't grieve. It means that you bounce back faster than your normally would.

An awakening will expand your awareness of your surroundings and nature around you. Taking long walks out in nature has never felt so good because you feel an almost supernatural connection with the earth and its beings. Many people have reported developing a 'green thumb' after an awakening while others say that they have a new desire to be vegetarians if only to reduce the harm they do to other creatures. You'll find yourself feeling more compassion for your fellow human being and becoming more charitable and loving.

After an awakening many people report heightened creativity. The awakening itself is akin to opening up the mind. Many people have a limited mentality that has been blocked by years of conditioning by nurture i.e. what your parents, teachers or leaders have told you. But an awakening clears away that old mentality and creates room for clarity of thought.

You may find yourself questioning every assumption you've ever made, every value you've held, or the way you've been doing things. This is a good thing because for one you'll stop accepting everything at face value and you'll seek a better understanding of the things in your life. This process of evaluation and observation can lead to the creation of entirely new and better ideas.

Many professionals have noticed that an awakening improves their work products too. Painters can see colors more vividly and come up with better art. Writers can write faster and better. Lawyers have better memories of laws and how to use them for their client's benefits. Regardless of profession, Kundalini awakening opens up your mind to be more creative and better at your job.

Kundalini awakening can also enhance your physical health and give you greater vitality. An awakening will leave your body feeling swifter and more decisive. If you're trying to get in shape, exercise will suddenly feel much more comfortable and more fun and exercise sessions will appear to fly by. Many people report increased sexual energy and libido.

If you're trying to develop better eating habits, an awakening is like cleaning up your palate so that your taste buds are more receptive to healthier, cleaner food. You'll probably find yourself developing a taste for fresh foods and vegetables and less susceptible to 'foods' that are dangerous for the body such as fatty, sugary and salty foods.

In general, an awakening will help you unlock your highest potential and thus your ultimate life. It improves your spiritual, physical and mental acuity beyond compare. You will feel healthier, look healthier and be healthier.

Can it be employed simply as a healthful practice?

The traditional yoga postures and stretches were always used to improve the flexibility of the body and prepare for the enlightenment of the Kundalini practice, however, it can also be used to enhance the body healthfully. Practicing certain moves, etc. that will awaken Kundalini in an individual purely to strengthen the body appears to be an inappropriate and wasteful use of these precise techniques.

Some trainers will guide the persons to properly practice Kundalini simply to illustrate Kundalini's benefits on well being, without touching on its spiritual effects. In reality, these are the ways yoga was introduced in other countries for many years. And although it is commendable to try to get better and encourage others to do so, sometimes a conflict of interest will arise between tapping any area meant to dissolve someone's ego and attempting to use that same energy to embrace an entirely ego-based purpose.

Chapter 4: How To Awaken a Dormant Kundalini

Close your eyes and take a deep breath. Try to quiet your mind from any thoughts. What do you feel at this point? One of the things that could have crossed your mind is your pulse. If things were hushed, you might just hear a slight buzzing which is the energy coursing through your veins and encompassing your muscles and enveloping your whole body. If you felt this way but don't know what it is or can't put a finger on a name, well then this most likely is kundalini.

By now, we know that Kundalini is a universally acknowledged and revered energy that exists in our lives. This coiled energy is awakened through Kundalini yoga, and those who practice it and subsequently release the coiled serpent from its slumber is said to receive spiritual enlightenment and a heightened sense of conscious awareness. Below, you can see the energy flow through the chakras when this stagnant energy is released and freed:

Those who awaken Kundalini energy are more creative, more inspired and balanced in spirituality, mentality, and mind. Since Kundalini is considered the life force that ignites everyday function of our minds and our bodies, it makes sense that we need to unlock this energy as it will only help us unveil our true potential and our creativity.

What's Yoga Got to Do with Kundalini?

Yoga was initially used as a path to enlightenment, but with more and more practitioners gravitating towards yoga as a stress and anxiety reliever, yoga's spiritual aspect was not fully embraced.

For those seeking out the spiritual practice of yoga, Kundalini is used as the yoga of choice. Instead of focusing on just the spirit or just the body or just the mind, kundalini yoga incorporates all these three elements into one holistic process that leads towards the release of energy. Regarding the physical aspect of the practice, kundalini yoga focuses on deriving the energy meridians or points where the energy flow is the best to heighten the awareness and activate specific areas such as the spine and the navel.

Essential breathing techniques are also vital, such as the pranayama that helps practitioners control their breathing and unlocking their energy. These physical attributes are done to achieve a higher state of awareness.

How to Awaken a Dormant Kundalini

Kundalini energy can be dormant for many reasons or no reasons at all. Just as how it comes to you, it can also leave. So how do you awaken a dormant kundalini? If you want to discover and awaken kundalini, here are 15 ways you can do that to facilitate and create progress in your practice:

1. Focus Your Breath

Breathing is one of the vital aspects of yoga practice of any kind. You may have gone off course with your breathing, and it could be that you got distracted. To get back on track is to do the most essential elements in kundalini practice to control your breathing. Focus on breathing towards the tail of your spine and then directing it upwards towards the crown of your head.

2. Focus on your posture

You are most likely sitting at least 70% of your waking hours, and this only leads to bad posture because we are sitting in the car, we are sitting in the office, we are sitting in meetings, and all of this makes us hunch or walk differently or sit wrongly and even sleep wrongly. Bad posture also prevents us from breathing correctly which is why in yoga practice, yogis and gurus always start a pose by telling to sit tall and keep our spine stacked.

3. Reject Negativity

Staying positive will help us improve and keep us objective and looking forward to our goals and tasks. By focusing on the positive aspects of our daily lives, we reject negativity and develop wholesomely in our practice, spirituality, and mentality.

4. Refine Your Diet

If you are trying to awaken your internal energy, we need to look at our practice holistically. Standing right, breathing right and staying positive also includes eating right, which means eating wholesome and healthy meals. Kundalini awakening also requires us to eat less meat. Over time, those practicing for years eventually eliminate meat from their diet. This is not a must, but it is encouraged. Eating the right foods helps keep you healthy and gives your mood an overall right complex.

5. Move Your Body

You can move your body in various ways, such as exercising, being one with nature, and doing physical work. Ideally, you want to move your body through the exercise you enjoy, which can be anything like long walks or bicycling or even jogging. Your body needs the movement which is why yoga incorporates asanas to pull, elongate strength and warm the body. There is no good keeping the body sedentary.

6. Stay Strong

It is good to stay healthy, but it is also good to accept and understand that not everything is within your will and control. There will be days that things will go amazing while there are days that things will go wrong and there are days that are just ok. Life is that way, but staying strong mentally helps you get through the darkest moments in moments of adversity.

7. Find Your Circle

Birds of a feather do flock together. We, subconsciously, mirror the people we are surrounded by and people we grew up with. Some of us having a pretty positive surrounding while some of us do not. The good thing is as we grow up, we can choose and create this surrounding by ourselves. We can consciously make decisions to surround ourselves with the people we want to be like, and this can be the kindest or the most honest, or the most successful. Our quality of life entirely depends on who we choose to be around with to attain our goals.

8. Get a Mentor

A yogi mentor is an excellent person to surround yourself with. You can have a deeper connection with your yogi and learn from them and share your Kundalini experiences. Part of this mentorship ensures that you have the right kind of support from someone who has experience.

9. Chant, Chant, Chant

Yogis rarely practice in silence. They usually chant and repeat mantras as it is a way of facilitating the Kundalini mood. Chanting is a great devotional practice to get your dormant Kundalini to revive itself and uncoil its energy. Join a group or find a teacher that you are comfortable with and repeats chants to help you rekindle the energy within you.

10. Activate Your Interests

In this busy and hectic lifestyle, we live in it is easy to get caught up and do only tasks and things that we feel we should not because we like it but because we think it's the right thing to do, or because it is expected of us or because we should do it. All this may deactivate the energy within you. To reignite it again, set aside an hour each day for yourself to pursue the tasks and things that you feel connects you back to your inner soul. Make this one hour an hour of your enjoyment.

11. Be here and be now

Be present to the situation and surroundings that your body is currently in as you go throughout the day. We need to be conscious of our surroundings and not to get caught up in a daze. Direct your focus by cutting out your extraneous thinking and instead live in the moment at hand. Mindfulness is what would also help revive a dormant kundalini and leave you feeling more grounded and satisfied.

12. Go with The Flow

Going with the flow is ideal especially if you have been organizing your life to minute detail. Sometimes it is great to let go and get rid of intense planning and instead, take each day as it comes. View your day as an adventure as opposed to a planned battle. If your day does not go as expected, keep positive and know that not everything is within your control.

13. Affirmations

While we are friendly and accommodating to the people around us, rarely are we kind to ourselves. Rarely do we take the time to take care of us because who else will? When we are always looking out for other people and not ourselves, our kundalini energy also suffers Take time out from your schedule to remind yourself of how beautiful life is, the things you are grateful for as well as your talents and attributes.

14. Cut Distractions

We often seek things that numb us such as binge-watching TV or browsing the internet or only looking at our cell phones. When our spirit has lost its direction, our energy also loses its compass. To awake the dormant kundalini, you can also start by not engaging with the people around you. You can switch off gadgets after 7 pm and only focus on yourself and your family. You can also distant yourself away from certain people for a certain period. Whatever you do, make a commitment to yourself that you want to eliminate distractions.

15. Try using music for relaxation

When you get into your asanas and meditations, putting on a flowing rhythm and music will promote your senses to get into a meditative state and assist in your kundalini awakening.

You do not want to rush and wake up a dormant kundalini overnight. Spiritual enlightenment is a gradual process of learning, healing, stepping back and understanding what it takes and how to get there. Kundalini is a practice, and it does not happen overnight. So be mindful of what you can do within a certain period and keep progressing from there.

Chapter 5: Kundalini And Yoga

The principles on which Kundalini Yoga was built are ancient, but still very relevant in the human experience today. Again, this spiritual energy starts at the base of the spine, and the process of awakening refers to how this energy spreads from your spine to the crowd of your head with time and practice.

The metaphysical aspect of the practices describes Kundalini as an awakening snake, emits an energy, or chakra that takes refuge in 7 locations in the body as you grow. According to methodology, the chakra energy rises through your being in the same way that air fills your lungs, then disperses oxygenated bloods throughout your body's vital organs as you exhale.

The goal is to ascend beyond the first 6 chakras and to access the 7th through what has been called, the "golden cord". This cord, as legend has it, connects pineal and pituitary glands. The significance of this is that those glands in particular are said to have been responsible for awakening a human being's conscious mind. And not just with Kundalini Yoga—these glands are the subject of enlightenment in many current and ancient teachings. To access them is to finally see yourself and the world as it is, rather than as you think or hope it could be. The golden cord, in this particular practice, is the key to your awakening.

Kundalini Yoga combines the old teachings of three other, more specific yoga related spiritual practices. Each yoga focuses on an aspect of the human experience, from devotion (Bhakti), to power (Shakti), and mental fortitude coupled with control (Raja). Each gives an avenue on which to pursue a high consciousness and help you exploit your creative potential. In this way, these practices are said to be a practical technology for the conscious mind.

In addition to harnessing the power currently resting within you, Kundalini Yoga is said to release the practicing individual from karma debt. If translated to western terms, being released from one's karmic debts is essentially the same as being forgiven for the mistakes you made throughout your life. It ensures that your soul is peaceful, and that even once you physically pass on, your soul will continue to be content. It is a fascinating concept, and is yet another spiritual benefit of Kundalini Yoga.

The Health Benefits of Yoga

There is a plethora of ways in which yoga benefits the body—too many to count. So, let's explore some of the different benefits of yoga in daily life.

1. Improves flexibility – This is one of the most fundamental benefits of yoga. You may not be able to touch your toes or bend all the way

forward in your first class, but you will notice over time that your body begins to loosen up, and with that will come a decrease in muscle pain as well.

2. Builds strength – Yoga is the best way to build a healthy amount of strength while balancing it with flexibility. Your muscles' strength contributes significantly to your posture, how you walk, and how you power the daily physical tasks that you may have. Lifting weights builds muscle too, but that (more often than not).

3. Improves posture – People underestimate the weight of their heads! When you slouch, the amount of tension your heavy had leaning beyond your spines center of gravity can have lasting effects. Yoga encourages and promotes healthy standing and sitting positions, so you will learn how to sit and stand properly which will increase the longevity of your back and neck especially.

4. Stops joint/cartilage breakdown – The body is more like a machine than anything else. Like most machines, it has to be well oiled and taken care of with great compassion. Your cartilage is a spongey substance that cushions the area between your bones within joints. Yoga takes you through full ranges of motion that will loosen those joints and promote your cartilage's proper maintenance. Without going through the motions, your cartilage will likely wear with age, and eventually will be scraped down until you're experiencing the trouble and pain of two bones rubbing together without any cartilage between them. Many elderly experience this, hence why they most so slowly. Yoga can solve this problem!

5. Spinal Protection – Spinal disks are the shock absorbers of your back, and require a healthy amount of movement to stay limber and effective. In yoga, many motions involve light twisting and turning to ensure that your spine stays healthy and supple through the years. Back problems affect millions of people, so it only makes sense to find a solution that can remove you from that statistic!

6. Promotes bone health – This is important for women especially! You've seen the commercials about the prescription pills that are supposed to combat osteoporosis. Well, this is a natural, much less rigorous way to prevent it. The stances and poses that you take in yoga help strengthen the bones of your arms and legs wildly, which is where osteoporosis likes to start. In addition to that, yoga as a whole helps to lower the amount of stress hormones produced in your body, which lowers the rate at which calcium is lost in your bones.

7. Blood flow goes up – Although yoga isn't the same as running or lifting weights, it is much more effective at evenly distributing oxygenated blood throughout your body. Going through the motions in a session promotes a higher blood flow to your body areas that may not always receive it as they should (hands and feet). A consistent practice will also lead to more oxygenated blood circulating healthily through your organs and tissues, and even help with people who have had heart or kidney problems and don't get the appropriate amount of blood to certain areas of their bodies. In addition to that, this increased flow reduces your chances of harmful blood clots.

8. Assists immune/lymphatic system – Everything in yoga from the contraction and stretching of a muscle, to transitioning between poses allows a fluid within immune cells to break free and "drain", if you will. As it drains, your body will be able to fight off infection more readily. It also makes it so that cancerous cells are broken down faster, and also so that the toxic waste within these cells is disposed of more quickly.

9. Improves heart health – Regularly increasing your heart rate during exercise can lower your risk of heart disease and the chances of depression because of the endorphins released during exercise. Yoga isn't an aerobic exercise by default, but variations can be done to simulate a situation where your cardiovascular fitness is challenged. And even for yoga that isn't ass vigorous, it still lowers your resting heart rate and improves your overall endurance.

10. Lowers blood pressure - If you have HBP (high blood pressure), you too can benefit from yoga. The constant movement combined with the cardiovascular challenge will regulate your blood pressure and eventually lead to an overall drop due to the consistent practice of raising and lowering it with different exercise forms.

11. Regulates adrenal glands – Cortisol is a stress induced hormone that appears when in a time of crisis, embarrassment, etc. Yoga reduces the amount of that this hormone sticks around. It first becomes present, it's helpful and makes you more alert, and even boosts your immune system. The real trouble comes when the situation that caused the increase passes and the cortisol sticks around. An overabundance of cortisol has been related to

depression, osteoporosis, HBP, and insulin resistance (leading to diabetes). It also has been said that a constantly uninhibited influx of cortisol can lead your body to a state of crisis, and in this state the body stores most things that you may eat or drink as fat for safety purposes. Nobody wants that!

12. Improves moods – It is no secret that any form of exercise improves your overall moods, and promotes a happier existence. The practice of yoga will promote an increase in those "happy" hormones like serotonin and the endorphins that fill you with joy, which can be a great combatant of depression.

13. Encourages a healthy lifestyle – There is a spiritual, mental, and physical aspect of yoga. When combined, these things will trickle into other areas of your life from eating to how you think act around others. Yoga encourages a heightened self-awareness, and in gaining an excellent appreciation for yourself, you will be more likely to begin taking better care of your wellbeing.

14. Improves focus – In yoga, there is no moment but the present one. The only way to master a pose is genuinely to focus within yourself, and to maintain that focus throughout your sessions. As your mind becomes accustomed to going to that present moment space, it will begin to show in other areas of your life as well, which can significantly improve things as small as driving to things as large as your professional career!

15. Relaxes your system – The relaxational aspect of yoga shifts the balance from engaging the sympathetic nervous system (fight or

flight responses) to the parasympathetic nervous system (relaxation, lowered heart rates, calmness).

16. Maintains the nervous system – With the mastery of yoga comes a level of bodily control that many can't fathom. There are yogis in the world that can harness the usually involuntary power of their nervous system and make voluntary changes, like lowering one's heart rate at will, or forcing blood to accumulate at a specific location in order to heal or even to incubate something (for women who want to create a healthier environment for pregnancy).

17. Releases tension – Our daily cause a lot of tension, and we don't even notice it! Everything from how you drive, to how you sit, to how you hold your face, and other subconscious actions require your muscles to operate in a certain way. Yoga will essentially help you to see where you hold tension, and in practicing you will also see it relieved over time.

18. Improves sleep experience – Along with the stimulation that comes from improved focus is the byproduct of the meditation that occurs during yoga. This byproduct of increased relaxation and decreased stress can also lead to more accessible, deeper sleep.

19. Grants peace of mind – Because of the level of inner peace attained after consistently practicing yoga, your general levels of sadness, anger, and frustration will go down. You will learn to live more in the moment, without taking things as personally or as seriously because you will learn that most of what stands before you cannot be controlled, and that your initial frustration comes from attempting to control it all.

20. Increases self-confidence – Many of us deal with the burden of thinking we aren't good enough. Yoga not only promotes the idea that you are good enough, but also that you don't need to be anything but who you are in this very moment. We live in a society of constant movement, and of chasing everything without being grateful for what you have. Yoga gives you a sense of gratitude for self, which will show in your future social interactions as confidence.

21. Assists in pain management – This can occur on a physical, mental, and spiritual level. On the physical level, yoga is great for those who experience joint pains, arthritis, and other muscle or bone related aches.

22. Grants mental fortitude – You will find that in staying dedicated to yoga, you will have gained a new level of discipline. Within this discipline lies a greater strength of mind, which most have said is the best benefit of yoga. This will translate to all other aspects of your life, and you will find that you can do more now on a social, professional, and sexual level than you ever thought you could.

23. Provides grounding – The trick to having a successful start with yoga is to find a good teacher. This teacher will essentially facilitate the beginning of your growth as a student of yoga, and will serve as a mental, physical, and spiritual guide for those who feel lost.

24. Replaces drugs with healthy habits – As you have read, you've seen now that yoga serves as a great, natural combatant to several diseases and ailments that can plague your life. Usually, each sickness comes with a list of pills that have to be taken in order to

suppress or maintain them. But one thing that you must remember is that yoga is thousands of years older than modern medicine, and yet the people who lived thousands of years ago, still will able to overcome overwhelmingly more powerful illnesses! So, rather than jumping on the prescription pill train, try implementing some yoga into your daily life and see how differently you feel. The only side effect of yoga is a happier, longer life!

25. Creates greater sense of self – In gaining a greater understanding of yourself and the world that surrounds you, you will begin to be able to dissect and pinpoint where your own troubles and challenges exist within your life. It is said that rage and hostility can be just as contributory to heart problems as poor eating and physical stagnancy. So, even if you are currently experiencing something that you don't want to experience, your new level of understanding about yourself will help you to figure out what the cause of your problem is, and to do everything within your power to remedy that situation within you.

As you can clearly see, implementing yoga into your life would bring nothing but goodness into it. Now, imagine these health benefits coupled with what Kundalini Yoga can do for you.

Skepticism is a healthy practice, although I would not suggest it here. When it comes to the spirit, there are no gimmicks; no tricks. There is only what works, and what doesn't, so if you really desire a greater quality of life as well as an even more powerful sense of self, this is the path for you.

Chapter 6: The Best Yoga Poses To Awaken Kundalini

Now for the part we've all been waiting for: the asanas (poses)! As I mentioned earlier on in the book, please remember that you should go at your own pace. If you feel like 10 minutes is enough for you each day that's wonderful and you'll get a solid base level introduction to practicing yoga. However, if you prefer to spend more time on each pose I highly recommend it.

As you get more comfortable do each pose that you've learned up until the day you are on. For instance, if you're on Day 5: do all poses 1-4 up until Day 5 so that they stay fresh in your memory and you can build on the flexibility you're developing with each pose.

Ready? Let's get started.

Day 1: Mountain Pose

This pose might look like you're just standing there, but if done correctly it serves a much greater purpose and is generally the starting position for other standing poses.

Step 1: Stand upright so that your big toes are completely flat and touching the floor. Keep your feet about hip width apart and parallel to one another. Now, flex your toes upward and wide—really stretch. This is going to gauge whether or not you're balancing your posture correctly. If you lose balance then most likely you're not centering your weight evenly on all points of your feet so you need to correct your balance so that it's spread evenly on your feet.

Step 2: Contract your thigh muscles and try to lift your kneecaps, but do so without contracting your lower abdomen. Lift the inside of your ankles to help strengthen those inner arches and visualize an imaginary line of energy that spreads the length of your inner thighs to your groin and then from your core (or torso) to your neck, head—all the way out exiting through the crown of your head. Now turn your upper thighs slightly inward and visualize lengthening the tailbone down to the floor while lifting your pubic bone toward your belly button.

Step 3: Now focus on pressing your shoulder blades back and then slowly stretch them out and release down your back. Lift the upper part of your sternum toward the ceiling without pushing the lower part of your ribs outward. Widen and stretch the collarbones, then hang your arms at your sides, palms facing forward.

Step 4: Finally, balance your head completely above the center of your pelvic area. Make sure that your chin is parallel to the floor and keep your mouth and throat soft as well as your eyes.

Stay here and breathe slowly and intentionally for 1 minute or however long you feel comfortable.

Day 2: Tree Pose

Step 1: First, stand in Mountain pose and begin to shift your weight a little bit onto your left foot. Keep the inside of the foot firm on the floor and bend the right knee. Slowly reach down and grab your right ankle with your right hand.

Step 2: Pull your right foot up and place it against your inner left thigh as high as you can to where it feels comfortable. Your goal should eventually be to press your right heel into your left groin completely flat with your toes pressing down toward the floor. Keep your pelvic bone directly over your left foot.

Step 3: Visualize lengthening your tailbone, getting it as long as you can. Press your right foot into your inner thigh and then place your hands in the prayer position in front of you, looking straight ahead.

If you don't want to put your hands in prayer position you can place them on your hips or at your sides.

Stay in this position for 1 minute, breathing evenly. After you've completed this, go back to Mountain pose and do Tree pose with your opposite leg.

Day 3: Bridge Pose

Step 1: Begin by lying flat on your back. Bring your knees up to a 90-degree angle and place your feet flat on the floor with your heels as close to your glutes as possible.

Step 2: Exhale while pressing your feet and arms firmly into the floor, contract your tailbone up toward your pubic bone and firm your buttocks muscles. Now lift your butt off the floor keeping everything parallel.

Step 3: Place your hands below your back on the floor either flat or you can clasp them together if that's more comfortable. Keep your abdomen muscles engaged and try to lengthen your back.

Step 4: Keep your chin lifted slightly above your sternum and your shoulder blades firm. To keep your shoulders from closing in, firm your outer arms and broaden the shoulder blades, stretching them across the base of your neck.

Stay in this pose for 1 minute and when you're ready to come out of it, do so by exhaling and rolling each of your vertebrae slowly down onto the floor.

Day 4: Extended Triangle Pose

Step 1: Stand in Mountain pose and as you exhale, spread your legs about 3-4 feet apart. Place your arms in the air parallel to the floor and then reach out to your sides, shoulders wide, palms facing down.

Step 2: Position your left foot slightly to the right and then place your right foot at 90 degrees. Rotate your right thigh so that it's facing outward and the center of your right knee is in line with your ankle.

Step 3: Now, exhale and bend your torso to the right placing it over your right leg. Do not bend at the waist, but rather at your hip. Strengthen your left leg and press your left heel into the floor. Rotate your torso to the left and let your left hip move forward a bit.

Step 4: Next you can rest your right hand however is comfortable—on the floor, your ankle, shin, etc. Now, stretch and raise your left arm up high to the ceiling lining it up with your shoulders. Be sure to keep your head neutral or you can turn to the left to look up at your left thumb.

Stay in this pose for 1 minute and then slowly inhale and come out of it by raising your arm toward the ceiling and pressing your back heel into the floor. Follow the same steps for your opposite side.

Day 5: Half Twist

Step 1: Sit on the floor with your legs flat in front of you. Bend your left knee and place your left leg over your right so that your left foot is resting on the floor at the edge of your right hip.

Step 2: Now, move your right foot over your left knee so that it's positioned outside of the thigh. Be sure to keep both sides of your butt evenly on the ground.

Step 3: Next you're going to lean back onto your right hand and then inhale while place your left arm over your head to lengthen your torso and spine.

Step 4: As you exhale twist to your right and bring your left elbow outside of the right thigh. Look over your right shoulder and be sure to keep length in your neck. As you continue to inhale try to lengthen your spine more. As you exhale, twist deeper into the pose.

Stay in this position, inhaling and exhaling for 1 minute. As you come out of the pose, do it on the exhale and release gently. Switch to the opposite side.

Day 6: Cat-Cow

Step 1: Start with both hands and knees on the floor. Be sure to keep your knees under the hips and wrists under the shoulders. Your spine should be neutral and back flat. Keep your abdominal muscles engaged and breath in deeply.

Step 2: As you exhale, round the spine upward as far as you can towards the ceiling. It helps if you imagine pulling your belly button into your spine. At the same time pull your chin into your chest and relax your neck. This would be considered the cat pose.

Step 3: When you inhale, arch the back and relax your stomach, keeping everything loose. Raise your head and tailbone upward making sure not to add pressure to your neck. This would be considered the cow pose.

Step 4: Flow back and forth from cat to cow for as long as you like, just be sure to connect the movements with your breathing and really stay conscious of each vertebrae as you inhale and exhale.

Again, you can do this for as long as you wish. It's a great spinal warming exercise and helps alleviate low back pain. I recommend at least 1 minute.

Day 7: Legs-Up-The-Wall Pose

Step 1: Determine the distance you need to be from the wall: if you're tall move farther away, if you're shorter get closer and adjust as needed. If you feel like this pose puts too much pressure on your lower back or you're uncomfortable, you can use a rolled up towel or a bolster to provide support in your lower back.

Step 2: Sit sideways and start with your right side facing the wall, as you exhale, swiftly bring your legs up onto the wall in one fluid movement and then slowly lower your shoulders and head onto the floor. If you feel like you need support at the base of your neck feel free to place a rolled up towel or wash cloth there to ease the pressure.

Step 3: Be mindful of the position of your chin—make sure you're not pushing it into your chest. Keep your shoulders pressed down flat towards the floor and place your arms out at your sides, palms facing upward.

Step 4: Keep the legs slightly taut to keep them from "drooping" and then sink the weight of your lower body down toward your pelvic floor.

Stay in this pose for as long as you like—it's exceptionally comfortable for getting into a meditative state. Just be sure that when you come out of the pose you're not twisting your back, but rather roll gently to one side instead.

Day 8: Cobra Pose

Step 1: Lie on your stomach in the floor with your legs out behind you and the tops of your feet touching the floor. Next, place your hands on the floor directly under your shoulders as you press your elbows back and into your sides.

Step 2: Place pressure on the tops of your feet and thighs and pubic bone as you press yourself firmly into the floor. As you inhale, straighten your arms and lift your chest off the floor. Make sure that you don't go so far that you're pubic bone is off the floor.

Step 3: Keep your shoulder blades firm as you "puff" your chest forward, lifting through the top of your sternum. Be mindful not to tighten your lower back. If you notice quite a bit of lower back pain or pressure, feel free to widen the distance between your legs as this should help.

Stay in this pose for 30 seconds as you continue to breathe slowly and evenly. On the exhale you can release.

Day 9: Standing Forward Bend

Step 1: Stand in Mountain pose with your hands on your hips. As you exhale, bend slowly forward at your hips. At the same time you should be drawing your stomach inward and engaging your abdominal muscles. You want to focus on lengthening your mid-section as you descend.

Step 2: Now, with your knees as straight as you can keep them, place your fingertips or palms on the floor in front of you. If this is too much of a stretch just grab wherever you can reach to—maybe your ankles or even your calves. Remember not to push yourself too hard.

Step 3: Press your heels into the floor and lift your butt into the air. As you inhale, focus on lengthening your mid-section. As you exhale release yourself deeper into the forward bend.

Step 4: Be mindful of your neck and keep it loose—let it hang freely.

Stay in this pose for 1 minute and then gently bring yourself out of it by unrolling your torso as you inhale.

Day 10: Extended Side Angle

This pose is somewhat similar to the Extended Triangle—the difference being that instead of both legs staying straight you will come down into a lunge position with the leg you're leaning into.

Step 1: Stand in Mountain pose and as you exhale, spread your legs about 3-4 feet apart. Place your arms in the air parallel to the floor and then reach out to your sides, shoulders wide, palms facing down.

Step 2: Rotate your right thigh outward and keep your kneecap in line with your right ankle. Now, you're going to roll your left hip forward and to the right, but make sure you're upper torso goes back and to the left.

Step 3: Firmly keep your left heel planted into the floor and as you exhale bend your right knee into a lunge position over your right ankle, making sure not to go past your toes. Try to aim for your right thigh being parallel to the floor.

Step 4: Keep your shoulder blades firm and extend your left arm up to the ceiling, turning your palm to face your head. As you inhale, reach your left arm over your left ear. Focus on stretching and lengthening your entire left side of your body. As you do so, look up at your left arm and also be mindful to lengthen your right side of your torso as well.

Step 5: As you exhale press the right side of your mid-section down onto your right thigh and press the fingertips of your right hand onto the floor. Your right thigh should be parallel with the floor.

Stay here and breathe for 1 minute, focusing on staying as open as possible. Reverse your feet and do the same thing for your left side.

Day 11: Camel Pose

Step 1: Get on the floor with your knees hip width apart. Visualize yourself drawing your glutes up into your body, but keep your hips soft while you plant your shins and tops of the feet into the floor.

Step 2: Place your hands on your hips as you rest your palms on your butt with your fingers pointing down. As you inhale, keep your shoulder blades pressed back and your head high. Ideally you want to keep your thighs perpendicular to the floor, but if you're a beginner it's perfectly okay to give yourself some slack. If you can't go straight back to touch your feet you can turn slightly to one side and place your hand on your foot, then go back to the neutral position and place your other hand on your other foot.

Step 3: Make sure to lift your pelvic bone upward and focus on lengthening your spine and releasing pressure. As you do so place your hands against your heels and your fingers pointing down to your toes. Don't squeeze your shoulder blades together and don't tighten your neck or throat area.

Stay in this pose for up to 1 minute, however long is comfortable to you. If you feel pressure in your lower back you can counteract this pose by going into Child's pose for a minute or so.

Chapter 7: Reaching the Higher Self

There are some traditions that divide humans into three selves: the younger, the middle, and the higher. Your younger-self is the subconscious mind. Your middle-self is your regular consciousness. Your higher-self is your god-self. The higher-self tends to be the trickiest for people to understand.

Some traditions view the higher-self as the best version that a person can be. Regardless of how you view the higher-self, the truth is that it is your god-self. The question to answer now is how you can connect with this god-self and how it can benefit you. The answer to this is simpler than you may believe. You can do this through meditation. During meditation, your mind becomes still. After you have cut off your inner chatter, it will create a path to realization and a connection with your higher-self.

This is the way that monks and gurus find their answers. They sit in meditation and allow their minds to become empty. In the end, you will come to the realization that you just know. This is how your higher-self works. Your higher-self always has a connection with the Divine and knows everything.

The younger-self is interested in elaborate rituals and things, while the higher-self wants to find serenity and silence. The more that you are able to quiet your mind, the more you will be able to manifest your higher-self. This is why meditation is one of the most important things you can learn how to do. You don't have to have an intention. All you have to do is allow things to unfold as they will. You will learn how to let things be.

Gaining Clarity

Meditation will allow you to naturally gain clarity and wisdom from your higher or divine self. You can follow any meditation practice that you want to as long as you keep up a regular practice. However, there are some meditation techniques that are designed with this in mind and used for the purpose of connecting with your higher-self. The meditation that we are going to go over is a great meditation for gaining more wisdom and mental clarity so that you can communicate with your higher-self.

1. Get into a relaxed and meditative position. Take a few deep breaths and allow yourself to relax.
2. Once you are relaxed, try to picture yourself as the best version of you. Try not to look at this on a physical level, but on every level, including spiritual, emotional, and mental.
3. Picture this version of yourself standing right in front of you, as if they are getting ready to talk with you. Remember that the person standing in front of you is a highly evolved person and can easily communicate

with you through telepathy, so make sure that you pay attention to any thoughts that may come to your mind.

4. Do your best not to try and force thoughts to come to mind. Allow thoughts to come in freely and without any pressure.

5. Turn your focus to your higher-self. Begin to communicate with your higher self in your mind. You don't have to speak out loud. All you have to do is think about the things that you want to say. Keep your mind open to whatever your higher-self tells you. Enjoy this conversation and make sure that you learn from it.

6. Once you have finished your conversation with your higher-self, take a moment to realize that this being you adore for all of its wisdom and brilliance is really a part of you. You are indeed fantastic. All you have to do is recognize the beauty that you naturally have.

7. On your next inhale, feel and watch as you breathe this higher-self back inside of you. While this happens, notice that everything that you love about your higher-self has now become a part of who you truly are. You are now your higher-self.

8. Take a few more deep breaths as you feel the brilliance and wisdom of your higher-self inside of you. Appreciate this newfound power. You are a beautiful and wonderful person.

When you do this meditation, you can make any adjustments that you feel are necessary to help it work for you. This is a great meditation to use when you want to connect with your higher self and to help you realize the amazing power that lives within you.

Chapter 8: Prana

What is Prana?

It is called by many names and terms, yet they all refer to the same divine energy: prana. Even some people claim so far that since prana is everywhere and that it cannot be destroyed, then perhaps prana is God. There are conflicting schools of thought on this matter, but the majority believes that prana only comes from God, but it is not God. Still, the nature of prana remains the same: It is everywhere; it is infinite; it cannot be destroyed but is transmuted from one state into another; and that everything – both visible and invisible – is made of prana. Without prana, then there is no life. From this perspective, it is not hard to say that perhaps prana, indeed, is God. However, this is something that you may have to decide on your own,

Understanding the Nature of Prana

Prana is said to be everywhere. It is inside you and all around you. No life can exist without prana. Prana is also in the breath. Hence, there is a famous practice known as pranayama, which is a practice of controlling one's prana by controlling the breath. Another nature of prana is that it cannot be killed or destroyed. Instead, it can only change or be transmuted from one state into another. It is interesting to note, that conventional science has also proven this teaching, that energy cannot be destroyed; it only changes.

Everything in the universe swims in an ocean of energy. Perhaps this is also how everything is said to be connected. Hence, the web of life.

Prana or energy can also be used for various purposes. It is not just for awakening the Kundalini. Many people use it for healing, such as in reiki and in pranic healing. It can also be used for many other purposes, even for evil. Indeed, prana is everything and everything is composed of prana. Although prana may be seen as one and the same, it should be noted that its quality might vary. When you use prana, only focus on harnessing positive energy.

There are many other ways to direct prana, although the simplest and usual way of doing it is by visualization.

Other known ways include dancing, chanting, and certain movements, among others.

Prana is considered important to humans. People with low prana are often more prone to getting sick, while people with lots of prana are more likely to be active and healthy.

Prana or chi has been in existence for centuries; in fact, ancient writings also talked about prana. Mind you, these writings can be traced back to before the time of Christ. However, although prana has been known and used for so long, it is not yet accepted by conventional science. Still, this does not mean that it is not real. Just because science cannot explain something does not mean that it does not exist.

Chapter 9: The Source, Akasha

Akasha or the source. It is believed to be the fifth element in which the four other elements originate from. It is the origin of all things. While it isn't technically an element, meaning you can't physically create it, it does possess all elements. It is most closely associated with the colors black and white. It does not conform to space or time. It is infinite. It is the beginning and the end. It's easy to see why many people associated Akasha with God. They are both described in similar manners, so it is perfectly fine to view Akasha as God if it helps.

Since Akasha possesses all of the qualities of the elements and holds all colors, mastering Akasha will give you the power to master the elements. This is by no means as simple as it may sound. To master this power requires a very high level of spiritual development and maturity. Still, it is something that can be done while you continue along your spiritual quest.

Just like the elements, everything in the Universe that can and cannot be seen comes from Akasha. Nothing is able to escape the power of Akasha because it is everywhere.

Some even believe that Akasha holds the records of everything that has happened or will ever happen of the past, present, and future. With a developed clairvoyant ability, a person can tap into the records of the Akasha and share somebody's future. Many psychics and diviners use this method.

Akasha lives within the astral plane. This is the reason for the spaceless and timeless ability of the astral plane. It's also important to know that every physical being has an astral counterpart. In fact, everything exists in the astral plane before they are given a physical body. Every plane is the same. They only differ in the types of vibrations that live within them. It's easy to understand that Akasha has the highest vibration of all the elements.

You do not have to master Askasha to benefit from its power. Mastery can end up taking years or your entire life to achieve, so it is important to start using its benefits now. When you start to work with Akasha, you will start to notice improvements in your psychic abilities, your chakras, and your energy overall.

Some practitioners do nothing but try to master the power of Akasha since it is the key to all things. However, gaining psychic powers and the like should not be your reasoning behind your spiritual focus. Gaining these powers is just a byproduct of awakening your Kundalini energy. You should focus on gaining spiritual maturity and not be blinded by gaining power.

Akasha is also sometimes referred to as intelligence. Whether or not this intelligence will help you or hinder you will determine your life; whether you become blessed or are someone who gets knocked around by life. Both types of people can easily be seen in life. Some seem to get everything they ever wanted and others who work their butt off but get nowhere. It is that person's ability, either unconsciously or consciously, to allow this power to influence their life.

A common practice that can be done to help Akasha work for you is to get up each morning before the sun rises and as the sun comes up, and before it passes at an angle of 30 degrees, look up to the sun and bow down to Akasha, thanking it for keeping you where you need to be. At another point during the day, anytime, look at the sky and bow again. Once the sun has set, look up at the sky and bow again. This isn't being done to a god or anything. This is being done for the empty space that has held you in place. You will be amazed how your life will change when you do this.

Without Akasha, just like without prana or air, you can't exist. It's easy to understand that without air you can't live. You need air to breathe. The vast majority of people don't even acknowledge the air around them, yet they are constantly using it. It can't be seen, but we know it's there. That is how Akasha works. We can't see it or touch it, but it is there and it is necessary for our survival.

In southern India, in the town of Karnataka, there is a temple dedicated to Annapoorneshwari. At the back of the temple, an inscription is written in Hale Kannada that describes how to design an airplane. It talks about how it should be constructed and it talks about how when the machine is flown, it will disrupt the ether. They believed that if the Akasha is disturbed, humans wouldn't be able to live peacefully. When Akasha is disturbed, psychological disturbances will become prevalent. This disruption has happened and we must live with it, but we can still use Akasha and actively work to improve ourselves with its power.

Accessing the Akashic Records

A person can access their own Akashic records without a lot of training or practice because they are their own. This is very different from accessing somebody else's, which takes a lot more practice and spiritual maturity. They can be accessed from anywhere and at any time. There are some directions that you should make sure you follow. When you do decide to connect with your own records, what is best for you will show itself. You don't have to have advanced psychic abilities to access your own records. All you need to be is alive and have a true heartfelt desire to get started. Lastly, you have to believe in yourself.

Accessing the Akashic records isn't something that only a few people are allowed to do, and as long as you have a pure heart, it won't be that difficult. Anybody can do it in many different ways. What plays the biggest part in this is the motivation behind it. If a person attempts to access the records out of mere curiosity, not to mention malicious intent, they will be misinformed or rejected. Curiosity comes through in many different innocent ways, like, "Let's see what my spouse was in a past life…" Accessing their records and learning about their past lives isn't going to help your relationship until you have come to understand who you are. You want to start with yourself.

I'm going to provide you with a quick practice to access your own records. Accessing your own is easier because you carry yours with you, so to speak. This means you don't have to access the hall of records that live within the astral plane. While it may not be difficult to access your own records, there are a few prerequisites. The first is being able to get into a meditative state. You have to know how to place your current thoughts to the side and be open to the information that you may receive.

Secondly, you must be willing to accept and reveal whatever is in your records. You can receive disturbing information from past lives and the like, so you have to make sure you are in a place where those things can be accepted. If you tend to avoid problems or steer clear of challenges in your daily life, how are you going to face this type of information in your records?

It's also a good idea to have a compassionate understanding of humanity so that your reading is meaningful. For example, you could learn that you were a slave owner in a past life. For most, this will be seen as a horrible thing, but that thought will close your heart and cause the reading to stop. Just because you were a slave owner doesn't mean you were a cruel person. You could have treated them fairly and kindly, but it was the norm for those times and you had very few options available to you. Having not moved past this past life could be what is affecting your current life. That's why it's important that you go into your readings understanding that past lives happen the way they do because of those times. The more understanding you have of life, the better your readings will be.

Having a bit of a ritual before your reading is always a good idea. Some preparatory meditation is great. It's also a good idea to voice your intention. Saying something along the lines of: "Allow the energy of truth and love to live on Earth. I would like my spirit guides to help me access my Akashic records so that I can have the wisdom to live my life with courage and awareness." Saying something with the words love, truth, and light will make it clear that you are doing this with love and without judgment. Truth lets the Universe know that you don't want to be given false information and that you are open to the truth no matter what it is.

It's very important that you have a reason for doing this and not just "let's see what I get" kind of attitude. You could end up receiving a lot of information that may not be influential to your current life. You want to be as clear and direct as possible.

To start, ask something along the lines of, "This (briefly describe your problem) is what I have been trying to work on, and I think there is more to it than what I know presently. If this is true, please send me information on how and when this problem started."

The way you get your answer will depend on your psychic strength. You could receive a video clip or picture on your vision screen. You could hear a clip of music that means something. You could taste, smell, or feel something. Or, you could just realize that you know something. It could also be a combination. Allow this information to come in and then ask a few clarifying questions if you need to. Once you are done, close the session with gratitude. You were given what you need to know in that moment.

You will want to have a journal and write down the things you learn immediately so that you don't forget anything. As far as knowing if it is accurate, you will just know. It will make sense to you. Sometimes people will experience changes, have pains disappear, and some experience a cold before they become better. These don't happen all the time or to everybody.

There may be times when the reading doesn't resonate with you, but it is still accurate. This is when you have received a reading has revealed an uncomfortable truth. Don't allow yourself to fall into denial. These readings can lead to big changes.

When you first do this, keep your readings brief. There is a lot of information in your records, so you must keep yourself focused. You don't want to end up overwhelmed. This can cause inaccuracy.

I also must caution you this, once you get used to access your own records, you could be tempted to access other peoples'. You should not do this EVER unless you have their explicit consent. Reading another person's records without their consent is like breaking into their house and stealing personal information. No matter how benevolent your reasoning may be, it's still wrong. Now, you can read family members' records without consent to the extent of what is relevant to you.

The most important thing is to make sure that you treat these records with respect because Akasha knows everything.

Chapter 10: Kundalini And Chakras

The base chakra is the beginning of the energetic journey in the subtle body. Its Sanskrit name means "root". It is the Earth element. It is survival. It is the right "To Have". It is here that the Kundalini energy is stored. This is the place of physical health, grounded-ness, stability, youthful quality, vitality, fight or flight instinct, and prosperity.

This chakra is associated with the color red. It is located at the base of the spine and contains the energy there and surrounding the legs, feet, and gonads. It is connected to your sense of smell, the first sense you are aware of when you are born.

When your root chakra is balanced, you will feel secure, abundant, comfortable with yourself, centered, calm, grounded, and connected to nature and the earth.

When your root chakra is imbalanced, you may experience feelings of insecurity, anger, disconnection, depression, shortage of patience, nervousness, greed, unnecessary fear, and lack. When this imbalance manifests in our physical bodies, it may appear as frequent illness, obesity, eating disorders, constipation, knee troubles, sciatica, and even hemorrhoids.

Since the root chakra is where the dormant Kundalini energy lives and rises from when awakened, it is important to recognize the qualities of the chakra and its connection to all the other chakras. However, one must not put all emphasis on this energy and here is why: Kundalini awakening begins here, but it may also end in the root chakra. Some experiences show that it can be the last chakra to awaken truly. The rest of the transformation through the chakras may occur first but in order for true balance to be achieved, the energy of Kundalini must return to the beginning to where the source of the energy awakening began.

The Second Chakra

The second chakra is also often called the sacral chakra. Its Sanskrit name means "sweetness". It is the element of Water. It is the place of emotion and sexuality. It is the right "To Feel". This is the place of pleasure, fluid movement, creativity, and passion.

This chakra is associated with the color orange and is located in the area just below the navel in your lower abdomen and is associated with the bladder, female reproductive organs, lymphatic system, and pelvis. It is connected to the sense of taste.

When your sacral chakra is balanced, you will feel happy, joyful, creative, passionate, and capable of connecting physically. This is also where the drive to procreate exists.

When your sacral chakra is imbalanced, you may feel unworthiness, isolated, numb, stiff, overly sensitive and emotional.

You may also have a sexual addiction, or alternatively what is called sexual anorexia, hormone imbalance, and potential for miscarriages or difficulty conceiving.

This is a place where you block your emotions. Here is where you can really restrict the flow of energy as a whole. It is important to do the emotional work necessary, recovering lost feelings and sometimes re-experiencing them, so that you can heal and release them as you continue your awakening journey. Ultimately, when you heal and unblock your sacral chakra, you can allow a healthy flow of your emotional energy so you can really experience pleasure through body movement and sexuality.

Unblocking your sacral chakra can allow you to experience change, growth, and connection with your passionate self.

The Third Chakra

The third chakra is also known as the solar plexus chakra. Its Sanskrit name means "lustrous gem." It is the element of Fire. It is power and it is energy. It is the right "To Act". This is the place of personal power, the strength of will, and sense of purpose.

This chakra is associated with the color yellow and it is located between the area just below the navel and the base of the sternum. The physical feature associated with the solar chakra is the adrenal glands. Your adrenal glands regulate metabolism, blood pressure, and your immune system.

When the chakra is in balance, you will feel energy and drive, confidence, sense of respect for others, as well as respect for the self, active and cheerful disposition, and a strong sense of purpose.

An imbalance of the solar plexus chakra can represent as an arrogant demeanor, demanding attitude, overbearing sensibilities, and addictions. The opposite side of imbalance would look like a deficiency of energy, a feeling of helplessness, a feeling of weakness, timidity, and submissive life approach.

This chakra demonstrates a significant turning point in Kundalini awakening as it will cause a profound shift in your intentions, intuitions, self-value and your ability to see beauty in the world. This is where judgment, biases, and prejudice melt away, first with the self and then the whole world around you. This is where you begin to feel your Kundalini power, but there is still so much more to go through.

The Fourth Chakra

The fourth chakra is also known as the heart chakra. The Sanskrit name for this chakra translates to mean "unstruck", or unhurt, unbeaten. It is the element of Air. It is love and relationships. It is the right "To Love". This is the place of compassion for the self and others, acceptance of the self and others, and balance in all relationships.

This chakra is associated with the color green and is located in the center of the chest, behind the heart and in the spine. The physical component to this chakra is the thymus gland and lymph system which help regulate immunity and help fight disease and illness.

When the heart chakra is in balance, you will feel love, compassion, interconnectedness, acceptance, life will flow smoothly, and there will be a general feeling of affection for everyone and everything- Universal love.

If the heart chakra is imbalanced, it can express this through excessiveness or deficiency. A deficient heart chakra can often look like low self-worth or low self-esteem, melancholy, isolation, depression, inability to breathe deeply. Excessive heart chakra energy shows itself in the form of co-dependency, clingy behavior and too much caretaking of others.

Interestingly, like with the extremes listed above, the heart chakra can spontaneously open for energetic flow from a newly experienced, deep love of someone, and on the other end, extreme loss or grief can cause a shift and crack open.

Regardless of what causes the initial awakening of the heart chakra, be it the Kundalini awakening process, falling in love, or grieving a loss, it is sure to be an emotional roller-coaster. This can be aided with the Kundalini practices outlined in this book.

The Fifth Chakra

The fifth chakra is also called the throat chakra. The Sanskrit name for this chakra translated is "purification." It is the element of Ether or sound. It is communication. It is the right "To Speak". This is the place of self-expression, speaking, soul song and the ability to communicate with others.

The color associated with this chakra is blue and it is located at the throat. There are several physical features connected to this chakra such as the already mentioned throat, jaw, and neck, thyroid gland, teeth, ears, and esophagus; everything associated with speaking and listening.

When this chakra is balanced, you can enjoy clear and truthful self-expression, honest and good communication, creative expression and affinity with self and others. There is also an ability to comprehend the balance of opposite forces with reverence, accepting the value of both light and dark, high and low and they each have a vital role in the harmony of all life energy.

When this chakra experiences imbalances or blockages, it can manifest as difficulty expressing oneself, inability to release wounds, pain or trauma because of suppressed emotions, sore throat, difficulty hearing, actual ear problems, tight neck and shoulders, and stagnant creative flow.

This chakra has a great deal to do with sound so a lot of the methods for clearing blockages, or opening and activating the throat chakra utilize singing or chanting, rhythm entrainment, and sound vibration.

The Sixth Chakra

The sixth chakra is often called the brow chakra or third eye. The Sanskrit name for this chakra translates to mean "perceive", or to know. It is the element of Light. It is visual perception, intuition, clairvoyance. It is the right "To See". This is the place of imagination, thought, telepathy, vision, rational logic.

The sixth chakra is associated with the color indigo and is situated between the eyes or behind the eyebrows. Its physical attribute is the pituitary and pineal gland. The pituitary gland regulates hormone secretions, while the pineal gland is involved in regulation of sleep patterns and circadian rhythms.

When the sixth chakra is balanced, there are great abilities in perception, your mind is at ease and can process thought quickly, improved memory and intelligence, lacking fear of death, you have a strong connection to your intuition and can have clairvoyant and telepathic abilities surface.

An imbalance in the sixth chakra can manifest as headaches, mental health issues and illness such as hallucinations and nightmares, paranoia, anxiety, and delusions. Because of its connection to sight and the eyes, it can also present itself as poor sight or visual perception.

Once this chakra becomes open and blockages begin to clear, energy can travel back down through the lower chakras for continued healing and cleansing, as there will likely be unresolved energy blocks still needing cleansing. That is why the Kundalini awakening process is an ongoing journey with the self.

The Seventh Chakra

The seventh chakra is also often called the crown chakra. The Sanskrit name for this chakra translates to mean "thousand-fold". It is the element of thought. It is expanded consciousness. It is the right "To Know". This is the place of understanding, of enlightenment.

The crown chakra is associated with the color violet and is located at the top of the head at the cerebral cortex. The physical component of this chakra included the brain, hands, nervous system and in part the pituitary gland, creating a link to the sixth chakra.

When the seventh chakra is balanced, you will have an expanded consciousness that will lead to a transcendence of barriers projected by humanity and the laws of nature, have a greater understanding and acceptance of death, mortality and the immortality of the soul, increased and heightened spiritual gifts and capabilities, and the creation of miracles.

If your crown chakra is blocked, it can manifest as migraines, headaches, and general tension around the head. You may also feel alienated or isolated, suffer boredom, have an apathetic quality, disconnection and a lack of comprehension or ability to learn and retain new information. It can also go in the direction of being a bit spacey, "in your head" all the time, and sometimes overly intellectual which can prevent your ability to attain pure-consciousness.

The balancing or opening of this chakra in Kundalini awakening is closely connected to the third eye. The ability to transcend and experience enlightenment is the moving away from smaller patterns to welcome a deeper, broader perspective, one that encompasses all life and all matter, beyond the confines of limited thoughts and beliefs that keep our kundalini locked and dormant.

From the Root to the Head and Beyond

The system as a whole is a beautiful, throbbing and constantly vibrating energetic life force of its own. This chakra energy is always present and always fluctuating. When the Kundalini energy is activated at the base of your spine in your first chakra, you begin the upward journey that will cause you to face all the elements, qualities, blocks, deficiencies and excesses of your chakras. It is the beginning of healing and awakening to your own divine light and energy to become one with the power of creation. What you discover on this path, the path through the chakras, will be how you come into contact with the true nature of yourself and all things.

Knowing about each chakra is important for the awakening process as it will give you the understanding to listen to your body. It is also important because they are the essential, energetic part of your being directly linked to Kundalini awakening experience. Take some time to really listen to each part of your body, each chakra system and develop a relationship to each energy so that you can be connected to the whole of your subtle body.

Chapter 11:
Enhancing Psychic Abilities

Psychic Abilities and How to Awaken Them

Clairvoyant forces can be grown normally. Everybody has an intuition, and keeping in mind that some have it more emphatically than others, we as a whole can wakeful that sense through training. Contemplation obviously is an extraordinary spot to begin. It's been said on numerous occasions that contemplation is useful for the psyche, body, soul, and in general prosperity. Putting in a couple of calm minutes independent from anyone else every day truly can help. Work on breathing methods too. Breath gradually done in an example that feels great to you. Add incense and candles to the experience too.

Keeping a diary is another smart thought for those keen on expanding their clairvoyant capacities. Record all that you experience during reflection. Record the majority of your emotions. Each picture or felt that goes through your brain may in the end synchronize with the world, so give nearer consideration to what your psyche is letting you know. The capacity to plainly picture occasions, individuals, and places in your inner being is an unquestionable requirement on the off chance that you need increasingly clairvoyant forces. Return and rehash your words frequently. In time, you should begin seeing the things you compose relating with genuine occasions.

A significant number of the stages are related with the intertwining of the enthusiastic, vitality body and the profound body, which is an imperative hidden piece of the advancement procedure.

1. Life Crisis

This stage doesn't really need to happen to everybody on the clairvoyant way in the event that they pay heed to the stones at a beginning time. Be that as it may, the move towards wishing to create on a clairvoyant level is frequently gone before by a real existence dramatization. This can be anything from a confounded adolescence to an ongoing separation.

2. Increased Awareness

This is the point at which you begin to see things out of the edge of your eye. This can likewise begin with seeing 'masses' of shading or whirling energies. For other people, it will be the start of hearing messages in your psyche, clear dreams, hunches, and thinking you are either going frantic or the brain is playing stunts. Frequently individuals disregard the stones here, and reject what their increased faculties are attempting to let them know.

3. Touchiness

Winding up progressively touchy to analysis and other individuals' perspectives. At this stage you start to realize that you can feel other individuals' sentiments. Perplexity and a feeling of, 'am I ordinary' win at this stage.

4. Looking

The quest for material that clarifies the peculiar encounters starts. This is frequently done discreetly through dread of derision. Likewise a powerful urge to discover 'similarly invested' people starts. It is at this stage you start to scrutinize your rational soundness truly! This is the final turning point. From this phase forward you will go through your time on earth looking for answers to life's inquiries. There might be rests in the middle of yet you will consistently be interested. It ends up like a tingle you can't scratch.

5. Beginning to support yourself

Be careful! The accommodating will abruptly fire going to bat for themselves and won't take any garbage. This might be present moment as it is just the beginning. A solid establishment has not yet been developed yet the wheels will have been gotten under way.

6. Feeling alone/misjudged

At this stage the creating clairvoyant has normally discovered material to halfway clarify their advantage and individuals of a similarly invested nature. Tragically at this stage, those frequently nearest to the individual will need to demolish their accomplice's/companion's new intrigue since they feel (however won't let it out) compromised by the new 'side interest'. The mystic will regularly be approached by a 'concerned' relative about how they are getting into a mysterious or being mentally conditioned, and how it is all gobbledegook. In the event that you don't have this stage you are extremely fortunate!!

This prompts a very befuddled mystic. Is it wrong to proceed? What would it be advisable for me to do? Am I distraught? Generally the choice is to continue discreetly and not impart the recently discovered learning to your quick friends.

7. I can't do it

Sentiments of uncertainty surface very well at this stage. The creating clairvoyant sees others moving at a quicker speed. They can't work out how to speed their own advancement however become progressively crippled due to the speed their mystic companions are moving at around them.

For some the inverse may occur, this will be they believe they are moving too immediately, alarmed by the experience and needing to back it off or shut it off in light of the fact that the duty feels overpowering.

Envision awakening into an abnormal and obscure world to you. On the off chance that you are one of the fortunate rare sorts of people who might be very inquisitive and would appreciate awakening in the new, the new would seem an overwhelming spot until you had became acclimated to it. For some, they start to wake up in this new world, they attempt to deny themselves the reality they are awakening some place distinctive in the expectation things can remain the equivalent, the recognizable and surely understood, 'safe place'. This will proceed until the creating clairvoyant is never again terrified and wishes to grasp the 'new world' they are awakening to – this can take a few while.

We have all sooner or later in our life dreaded change. The stunt in defeating the dread of progress is to pause for a minute to quick advance life to how it will be on the off chance that we continue as before. Life can't change except if we change, only trusting it will change prompts dissatisfaction. In your brain, quick forward your life to how it will be once change has occurred. You will before long observe change is an energizing alternative!

8. Needing quiet/to be distant from everyone else

The faculties are as yet honing, as they are doing so it is likely at this stage the creating clairvoyant turns out to be exceptionally delicate to boisterous commotions, they may discover they can't stand the radio playing or the sound of raised voices. Regularly they will need to be in open space or feel a solid should be in the farmland. An expanded wish to spend periods alone considering or 'gazing out the kitchen window.' Your body is revealing to you it wishes to ponder. During this stage it is important to locate an ordinary calm spot during the day to maintain a strategic distance from touchiness.

9. Acknowledgment that your activity/conditions are not directly for you

This is the start of figuring out how to see the blocks!! Frequently individuals will hold up until they are made excess or sacked (the stone) before they can see they have outgrown their activity/conditions/relationship or that their work environment or home doesn't coordinate with their freshly discovered mindfulness. This is regularly a shocking stage since it is tied in with understanding that your life has frequently been a trade off (not generally) up until this point. The troublesome piece is the mental fortitude to give up and proceed onward.

Traveling through this stage regularly turns into a hindrance for a great many people and postpones their advancement. This stage is tied in with splitting ceaselessly from the choices 'made for you' throughout everyday life and 'what you have done to satisfy another'. It is tied in with breaking free of the vocation you picked in light of the fact that it satisfied your folks, the relationship you remained in for accommodation or the activity you do, for the cash.

Likely the most significant factor in picking the mystic way and building up your expertise as well as could be expected; is about genuineness. You can't be a genuinely bona fide mystic except if you are straightforward with yourself. The individuals who are not fair with themselves regularly dread the clairvoyant way. The individuals who are straightforward with themselves grasp it!

10. Feeling deserted

This part doesn't really happen to everybody on the mystic way.

At this stage loved ones begin to leave your life or they seem, by all accounts, to be leaving. The creating mystic never again feels associated with those they have been partner with for quite a long time. A mind-blowing structures start to break down. All that you thought to be genuine/are connected to, self-destruct.

How discouraging!! This is really a fabulous stage, giving you ensure you stretch your view past the present circumstance. How would you fix a neglected structure? Well you don't! First you need to wreck it with the goal that you manufacture another, more grounded one in its place.

This stage is tied in with seeing through any hallucinations. Through this stage we find what is genuine. We genuinely reveal to ourselves lies! We let ourselves know all is well when it's most certainly not. We disclose to ourselves it's terrible when obviously it's alright. At the point when all is detracted from us we start to comprehend the excellence of the Universe. We build up an extraordinary comprehension of what is extremely significant and figure out how to profoundly welcome the little things throughout everyday life. Incidental data progresses toward becoming random data once this stage is finished. What appeared to be wrecking doesn't convey a similar feeling it did beforehand.

Wild weeping for no obvious explanation is a piece of this stage. This is on the grounds that the cells of the body are beginning to lose old memory, clearing a path for the solid capacity to see into your very own and other individuals' lives.

11. Expanded capacity

The clairvoyant faculties more often than not at this point are creating with a generally excellent and firm establishment. The capacity to 'read' individuals is regularly actually very solid by this stage.

12. De-tox

This phase for certain individuals comes from the get-go, for other people, it comes significantly later. In the event that you are overlooking it a physical ailment will frequently need to surface to demonstrate to you (a stone). The period of time you have been disregarding the need for this the heavier the physical sickness.

At this stage the time has come to tidy up your body and on the off chance that it has not occurred as of now, your musings. As the capacity to channel higher energies than your own, builds, it is fundamental the channel the energies are utilizing, is a 'spotless' one. In the event that it isn't, as happens with a ton of mystic's not decent physical disease starts to happen. On the off chance that you decline to de-tox, the impact is somewhat similar to stuffing a potato up a fumes pipe.

To de-tox means fasting for a couple of days. There are a wide range of fasts you can do, from just drinking water for a day or somewhere in the vicinity, to having dark colored rice for breakfast, lunch and supper for as long as ten days. Do a colon rinse, eat a lot of crisp products of the soil. Eat less sugar and meat. Limit your caffeine admission. Avoid low vitality nourishment, for example, takeaways and microwave suppers. In the event that you smoke, drink a lot of liquor or are dependant on any type of medications (lawful or illicit) at that point either stop or get help to stop.

Kindly note, ingesting unlawful medications is a low vitality practice; in this manner adverse to yourself as well as any individual you might peruse for. Because of the reality it is a low vitality act, you will draw in low vitality soul, and you won't have the option to continue your vitality at a sufficiently high vibration to channel effectively. It would be an over the top bounce from being low vitality to directing high vitality. Long haul, individuals who do this will cut off the lights will blow!

13. Needing to support everybody

This stage may seem as if it is an extraordinary spot to be. In established truth it isn't. You can't support anybody, just yourself, you can offer individuals an 'advantage' not a 'hold up'. On the off chance that you attempt and drag an individual along to a spot inside where they truly would prefer not to be nevertheless you think it is best for them, stop it – disregard them!! Concentrate on 'oneself', your 'self'. Individuals are fine as they may be, you just reserve the option to change yourself – disregard them!

Those in your life be that as it may, may oblige it for some time to be well mannered. Because you have begun to locate this newly discovered information you figure the world should know, you will in case you're not cautious, get the 'crackpot' status inside your family or friend network. You reserve no privilege to smash things down the throat of others. On the off chance that they are intrigued they will inquire. In the event that you do slam information down individuals' necks (there will be the allurement) be readied on the grounds that at some stage you will get your speculations shot somewhere around the 'life is just what you can see' doubter. In the event that/when you get to this stage, contending may be a misuse of your vitality. Acknowledge and watch their perspectives as they may be, they're qualified for them. You wouldn't care for your assessment shot down so it's out of line to take shots at or back at theirs.

For the most part at this stage the creating mystic concerning this subject won't be tremendously certain inside oneself. You will know when you are, on the grounds that you won't have a need to advise others how to be, and they will start to have a profound regard for your enthusiasm for clairvoyant improvement. It's practically unexpected in that regard.

This stage is a trial of how consistent with yourself you are. Hardly any individuals like to be 'lectured' on how they should carry on with their life, so recollect LEAVE THEM ALONE, regardless of the amount you can see they are going along an inappropriate way. Offer exhortation ONLY on the off chance that they inquire! Stay away from the, 'let you know so' when they've committed their error. In the end they will approach you first for your mystic exhortation before they act (keep it unprejudiced) when they have seen a couple of times, your expectations have been exact. Meanwhile, center around proceeding to create yourself.

14. Know all

At this stage you 'know everything'. The creating mystic ends up exhausted with the techniques they are learning. Feel their gathering is keeping them down; they don't have anything more to learn. The conviction begins to set in that they have encountered enough to proceed onward and go only it, away from their companions.

A few people lose companions in this stage and become seen as aloof, regardless of whether on knowing the past they are believed to be all knowing. As this stage turns out to be progressively built up, the clairvoyant gets to the phase of 'the more you realize the less you have to state', inevitably increasing extraordinary regard for their capacities as the need to lecture vanishes – an incredible spot to be.

15. Clearing

This is the stage the fun truly begins!! The clearing stage is the point at which every one of the things you have never managed, or every one of the things you discover startling, start to raise their head. Your extremely most exceedingly terrible feelings of trepidation become substances and every one of your weaknesses pound at you. The more you have overlooked them throughout everyday life, the more articulated the manner in which the Universe will indicate them to you for clearing. The path forward with this stage is to grasp and respect the clearing stage, for this is the thing that will truly transform yourself for the better until the end of time!

This stage as a rule includes a great deal of crying and outrageous' of feeling. During this stage it is regularly best to remain with your present occupation and conditions. The very underlying foundations of what you thought was steady will be shaken. It is regularly at this stage the creating mystic thinks they have to change the facades (Job, relationship and so forth) to satisfy them. This isn't the situation, accusing these circumstances, as the wellspring of your despondency will slow the procedure. Stick with 'preparing' the emotions you are experiencing, at exactly that point change the facades if your sentiments are as yet the equivalent.

Contingent upon the creating mystic, this procedure can last a few while and will occur pair with a portion of different stages. During this procedure, the creating clairvoyant will acknowledge it's anything but a maverick's procedure and come back to their companions inside their advancement bunch for assistance and counsel.

16. Leap forward

After the clearing procedure (which can take some time) the mystic turns out to be especially insightful. They can 'see' what is happening inside/for somebody at a hundred paces. This is on the grounds that anything that was impeding opening up to a genuine condition of being, has been expelled during the clearing procedure. There is then nothing halting you!!

Chapter 12:

Astral Travel and Clairvoyance

Astral travel is defined by some as the ability to have an out of body experience voluntarily. This concept theorizes that they soul is capable of traveling around outside of one's physical body, that the soul cannot be trapped within one's physical form and may be projected at will. Most people experience astral travel during near-death experiences or during times of great illness. With the enhancement of psychic abilities, it is entirely possible to perform astral travel at will. Astral projection usually only lasts for a few hours, though it may feel much longer (more like days or months) to the one who is experiencing astral projection.

Astral Travel is often described as "dreaming while awake", and many consider this concept to be like having an out of body experience. Astral travel is your mind's ability to experience your surroundings without being limited to your physical body. Astral travel allows your soul to be free from your physical body in order to travel the universe freely. While experiencing astral travel, you control the astral projection's length of time. During astral projection, you remain in control of your mind and are therefore able to steer yourself away from any source of negativity that you may encounter. The ability to see and communicated with those who have passed away is not an uncommon experience during astral projection, and those who are able to achieve astral travel are also able to visit various countries, planets, and even other realms during their projections.

An individual's soul or astral body is said to be connected to the individual's physical body by an astral cord (also known as the silver cord) that can stretch to an almost infinite length. The silver cord cannot be severed, with the only exception being in the occurrences of death.

1) Sitting in a quiet environment and in a relaxed position, perform meditation in order to relieve all tension and stress from your body.

2) Lie on your back on a completely flat surface, and close your eyes lightly.

3) Remain relaxed until you hear or feel the vibrations often experienced during meditative exercises. Keeping your eyes closed, imagine your astral body rising out above the limits of your physical body.

Clairvoyance (Psychic Vision)

One of the most popular forms of psychic ability is clairvoyance, and (especially in books or television) it is often referred to as "the gift". The ability of clairvoyance originates within the sixth chakra (the Third Eye) in the areas of the brain biologically recognized as the pituitary and pineal glands. While everyone has the ability to possess some psychic ability, not everyone will have the same ability to be a clairvoyant individual. The majority of individuals are born with relatively strong clairvoyant abilities, but most people lose these abilities by a certain (often young) age. This can be demonstrated when children claim to see deceased relatives (even those whom they have never met), when they have seemingly realistic "imaginary" friends, or when children seem to intuitively know when something is wrong with the adults surrounding them.

Clairvoyance is defined, simply, as the ability or skill of psychic vision. A more in-depth definition of this skill can be described as "perceiving things or events in the future or beyond normal sensory contact". Clairvoyance is sometimes referred to as "second sight" or "psychic sight" and translates to meaning "clear seeing". This skill is described by those who experience it as the reception of intuitive clues, often in the form of symbols, images, or visions. Some clairvoyants claim that certain tools are able to help them in order to easily connect with or strengthen their abilities: the more common tools for this purpose are tea leaves, tarot cards, runes, or even crystals. Precognition is a form clairvoyance in which an individual is able to foresee events before they happen. Precognitive abilities usually present themselves as visions while one is asleep.

Chapter 13:

Activate And Decalcify Your Pineal Gland

The pineal gland or your third eye holds remarkable power. However, only a few people can tap into this power and use it effectively. Many people simply have an underdeveloped third eye. But, the good news is that there are exercises that you can do to strengthen your third eye so you can start using and enjoying its immense power. Let us discuss them one by one:

- *Who is it?*

This is something that you can do every time your phone rings or beeps. Simply ask yourself, "Who is it?" Pay attention to what you see in your mind's eye. Do you see any image or impressions? Be open to receiving messages. This is how you can connect to your intuition. You should also realize that you have a strong intuition and that you only have to learn to connect to it. Of course, this technique is not limited to calls or texts on your phone. You can also adjust it a bit and use it in other ways. For example, if you hear a knock or any sound at night, you can ask, "What is it?" and pay attention to any messages that you get from your intuition. The important thing is to start connecting to your intuition once again.

- *Forehead press*

This technique is becoming popular these days. This, however, does not work on everyone but it is still worth trying. This will allow you some specks of prana in the air. They usually appear as little dots or any form of white light. The steps are as follows:

Place your index finger in the area between the eyebrows where the Ajna chakra is. Press it gently and maintain pressure for about 50 seconds. Slowly remove your finger, blink your eyes around five times, and look at a blank wall. Just focus lightly and try to see with your peripheral vision. Do you see little dots or any specks of white light? This is prana in the air.

To help you see the energy, you might want to do this in a dimly lit room. Look at a wall with a neutral background. This is a good way to use your third eye to see energy, but it is not a recommended method to strengthen the Ajna chakra. Still, this is something that is worth trying, especially if you just want to see prana.

- *Visual screen*

This is a good technique to use for visualization exercises. To locate the visual screen, close your eyes and look slightly upward. With eyes closed, look at the area of the Ajna chakra. This is your visual screen. You can project anything that you like to this screen, especially images. You can consider this as some form of internal magic mirror.

The main purpose of this visual screen is for your visualization exercises. Here is a simple exercise you can do to increase your concentration and willpower:

Assume a meditative posture and relax. Now, look at your visual screen. Imagine an apple floating in front of you. Now, just focus on this apple and do not entertain any other thoughts. This is just like the breathing meditation. However, instead of focusing on your breath, focus on the apple in your visual screen.

When you are ready to end this meditation, simply visualized the apple slowly fade away and gently open your eyes.

You are also welcome to use any other object for this meditation. If you do not want to use an apple, you can visualize an orange or even an elephant. The important thing is to have a point of visual focus for this meditation.

- Charging with the fire element

Remember that the intuition is associated with the pineal gland, in the pineal gland is the third eye chakra. Now, this third eye chakra is associated with the fire element. Therefore, you can empower your third eye chakra by charging it with the element of fire. This is a powerful technique so be sure to use it carefully. The steps are as follows:

Assume a meditative posture and relax. Close your eyes. Now, visualize the brilliant and powerful sun above you. This powerful sun is full of the element of fire. As you inhale, see and feel that you are drawing the energy from the sun. Let the energy charge your third eye chakra and empower it. Do this with every inhalation. The more that you charge your third eye, the more that it lights up and become more powerful. Have faith that with every inhalation, you become more and more intuitive.

Keep in mind that this is a powerful technique. If you are just starting out, it is suggested that you only do up to 10 inhalations in the beginning. You can then add one or two more inhalations every week. You will know if you can execute this technique properly because you will feel pressure on your forehead in the area of your third eye chakra. Take note that you should not just visualize your third eye chakra getting stronger, but you should also be conscious that your intuition becomes more powerful the more that you charge your third eye. The power of visualization should be accompanied by your intention.

Note

It should be noted that the Ajna chakra and crown chakra are closely connected. If you want to improve your intuition, it is only right that you also work on your crown chakra. Of course, this does not mean that you should ignore your other chakras. Again, the whole chakra system is important to your spiritual development and to the awakening of the kundalini.

Conclusion

Thank you for making it through to the end of Kundalini Awakening, let's hope it was informative and able to provide you with all of the tools you need to achieve your goals whatever they may be.

The next step is to continue your practice and see where your path leads. The exercises in this book are rooted in an ancient and mysterious past of Indian culture. They literally could be practiced for years without finding an end. Even the simplest meditation exercise can be practiced for decades without losing its potency and power. This shows the immense amount of potential that humans have to transform their lives and empower themselves that these practices have to offer.

The next step is to reaffirm every day that you are on your way to becoming a better, fuller you. Believe in yourself and your ability to make the changes necessary to realize your goals. Once you've removed the clutter from your mind, you will turn overthinking into focused achieving, each and every day. You may have heard many times over, "easier said than done." Well, you should be excited to learn how to do what you set your mind to do. You've wanted to make a change for a long time. Taking the steps to make your goals come to fruition is something many people never achieve.

It is times like this, after having taken a big step forward in my life, when I begin to reflect on how far I've come. It is hard to appreciate your progress sometimes when you are in the heat of battle and struggling every day during the beginning, middle, or even near the end of your efforts. There is nothing better than stepping up onto that final rung and looking down to see all of those completed steps in your wake.

Remember when you were sitting at square one, unable to free yourself from the chains of overthinking? I know it well—I've been there myself. It takes a great deal of courage to stand up and say, I'm ready to make a change. It saddens me to think that many people continue to overthink and overanalyze throughout their entire lives, missing out on the experiences and appreciation that a free mind can realize. It is easy to slip into the comfortable habits of mindless eating, checking a phone or tablet every few minutes, and going to bed later and later until your system is all out of sorts. Sometimes, it seems too easy to give in and let what's easy overshadow what's worth working for. You don't have to be a slave to overthinking, and maybe it's possible for you to take what you've learned and help change lives around you.

Perhaps you know someone who seems to be struggling with overthinking, stressing out about everyday challenges and stress just like you were at the beginning of your journey. Consider reaching out and sharing what you've learned. Nothing feels better than sharing new knowledge with someone who can use it to make the positive changes you've seen happen in yourself. Maybe it's a coworker, a spouse, or a close friend. Many people from different walks of life will benefit from the changes laid out in this book, so why not share your story!

www.ingramcontent.com/pod-product-compliance
Lightning Source LLC
Chambersburg PA
CBHW070920080526
44589CB00013B/1379